Real Estate - For Sale by Owner
by Kevin Knowlen

Real Estate - For Sale By Owner, LLC

Authored by: Kevin Knowlen
Edited by: Sharon Olson
Cover designed by: Ella Lee

ABOUT THE AUTHOR

Kevin Knowlen is the author of the book Real Estate - For Sale By Owner, and the owner of Real Estate For Sale by Owner, LLC, a limited liability company through which Kevin advocates and teaches methods to homeowners on how to sell their own home, often avoiding some of the typical real estate sales commissions. Kevin actively presents selling strategies in seminars to coach people as they plan and work through the process of selling their own home.

LEGAL DISCLAIMER

The author is not a lawyer. The following information does not constitute legal advice and is provided solely as a reference. Also, real estate rules vary from state to state. Engaging in a real estate sale is a legal transaction and your legal interests are affected. You are is encouraged to retain counsel to protect your interests.

Legal topics in this book have benefited from input from Russell C. Leffel, a Kansas Attorney, who emphasises that as a reader you should engage an attorney in your state to help you protect your own legal rights and interests.

Text copyright © 2014 by
Real Estate - For Sale By Owner, LLC
All rights reserved

To my lovely wife and kids for their endless love and support, thank you wholeheartedly for supporting me during the course of writing this book. To my mother who spent tireless hours editing and suggesting improvements to the book: I appreciate your support, kindness, and loving touches you put into the book. Throughout the course of writing this book there were multiple setbacks and interruptions, thank you to all of those who helped me refocus my attention.

Table of Contents

Introduction 1
Step One: De-Clutter 7
    Kitchen & Dining Room Clutter: 10
    Living Room Clutter: 12
    Bathroom Clutter: 14
    Bedroom Clutter: 16
    Garage Clutter: 18
Step Two: Repair 20
    Caulking: 21
    Plumbing and Fixtures: 23
    Furnace: 25
    Flooring: 26
    Good Working Order: 28
Step Three: Staging 29
    Kitchen: 31
    Dining Room: 33
    Living Room: 35
    Bathrooms: 37
    Bedrooms: 38
Step Four: Price 40
    Hire an Appraiser: 41
    Do Your Own CMA: 42
    Use Zillow: 45
    Tax Appraisal: 46
Step Five: Pictures 49
    Hire a Real Estate Photographer: 49

Take Your Own Photos: 50
Take Your Own Video: 51

Step Six: Advertise 53
Listing Service: 54
Zillow: 56
Facebook: 57
Craigslist: 58
Open House: 59
Signage: 61
Newspaper: 62

Step Seven: Show 63
Lock Box: 63
Sign-in Sheets: 64
Home Fact Sheet: 65
Business Cards: 66
Checking on Real Estate Agent Credentials: 67

Step Eight: Offer and Acceptance and Contract 72
Offer and Counter-offer: 73
Contract: 74
Addendums and Disclosures: 76
Pre-approved Finance Letter: 79
Home Inspection: 79
Radon Test: 80
Foundation Inspection: 80
Bank Appraisal: 81

Step Nine: Title and Closing 83
Title Company: 83
Loan Payoff: 85
Buyer's Closing Costs: 85

Seller's Closing Costs: 86
Final Walk-thru Inspection: 87
Receipts: 87
Day of Closing: 88
Concluding Thoughts..91

Real Estate - For Sale By Owner

Introduction

Are you interested in selling your home by the For Sale by Owner (FSBO) method but you are unsure of what is involved? Do you want to save money on the typical real estate sales commission of 6% but worried that you might miss one of the steps involved with the whole real estate transaction? Are you worried about missing out on services that real estate professionals provide and that you are missing information on how to sell your home yourself? Wouldn't it be great if someone wrote a book about how the entire process of selling your home works, which makes it easy to understand most of the aspects of selling your own home?

If you answered yes to some or all of the questions above, then this book is for you. This book will teach you most everything you need to know about what's involved with selling your house, enabling you to save money on the typical real estate sales commission of 6%, and yet get all the benefits and services a real estate professional normally provides. Reading the steps in this book will prepare you for listing your property for sale and the actual sale of your home. I cover many of the Do-It-Yourself aspects of preparing your home to sell, listing it on common websites that real estate professionals use, and finally the steps leading up to the closing. Using these methods, you can save thousands of dollars in the course of selling your home. I do my best to explain things in sufficient detail, so that you can gain the confidence you may need for selling your own home. I cover topics like how to show your home, how to interact with real estate professionals who show your home, and what to do after you receive an offer. I also explain in detail what a typical real estate transaction involves, from the offer to the closing. Be assured that after reading this book, you will likely feel comfortable with the entire process, and will likely feel confident in selling your home, which can lead to you saving thousands of dollars in real estate sales commissions. By learning the methods and practices I write about you can do many of the tasks involved in selling your own home, and still have real estate professionals on your team. Reading this information will help you determine what you are capable of doing yourself and give you bargaining power to save on typical commissions. From knowing these principles in this book, you will learn that you could hire a flat-fee real estate professional (selling agent) for as little as $600. This amount will provide you some but not all of the services that you would expect to get from a full service selling agent. I explain throughout the course of this book the aspects that are great for do-it-yourself and which aspects you should involve a flat-fee real estate agent or other professional.

    You might feel that that's a bait and switch considering the title of the book, since I am still saying that you should real estate selling agent—that if you hire a selling agent, is it really FSBO? To ease the mind of the reader, yes this is still a book about FSBO. This book is about you taking charge, and controlling the entire process of selling your own home. But let's recognize that FSBO does not necessarily mean that you have to do everything yourself. For the purposes of this book, we will use a loose definition of FSBO that includes using some services that are provided to the seller by professionals, but at the seller's discretion. Selling your home is a legal transaction and you should hire professionals along the way to ensure that the transaction is handled properly. This might or might not include a real estate professional or a real estate lawyer. The point I make is that it is up to you whom you hire.

According to the US census bureau (https://www.census.gov/construction/nrs/pdf/uspricemon.pdf), the average sales price for homes sold in the U.S. in April 2014 was $320,100. If you were to pay the typical 6% commission you would pay a total of $19,206 at the closing of your home. Under this scenario the seller agent's company and the buyer agent's company would split the commission, each company getting $9603. This could represent 1-5 years of home value appreciation depending on your area and the years involved. Although real estate professionals will work hard for your business, and they do provide you a service for a fee, for some homeowners it might be in your best interest to partake in a portion of selling your own home and negotiate some or all of the commissions involved with the transaction.

I was a homeowner just like you who decided it was too expensive to hire a real estate professional as I did not have enough equity in my home to share at the going rate of 6%. I could not sell my home in the traditional manner and needed to cut corners. I realized when I began to sell my house on my own that I had many fears—the same fears you may have. I had questions that needed answering. Some of the questions stemmed from the fact that I didn't know how to show my house. What happens when a real estate professional calls and wants to show my house? How do I know that they are real estate professionals and not just somebody else? Some of my greatest fears were once someone makes an offer, what do I do next, how do I accept an offer and move toward closing? These things were all so obscure. I was worried about legal implications, and about addendums and disclosures. I didn't know if I should I hire a lawyer to handle these for me or what to do. I want to reassure the reader that you will discover the answers to these questions in this book and the mystery of selling your own home won't seem so elusive. I have personally navigated through the processes of selling my own home and I write this book to share my experience gained in doing so.

There is a companion website to this book at http://www.realestate-forsalebyowner.com where you can watch webinars, view pictures, find examples of concepts, and print checklists. There are also various other tools and resources on the website that can assist you in your do-it-yourself home sale.

I have designed this book to be read from start to finish. It starts with the basics about how to prepare your home for sale, then describes how to price your home and market it. Finally it describes the processes involved from an offer to the closing. If you read and follow the process I advocate, then I am certain that you will successfully sell your home while saving possibly thousands of dollars. The book is laid out according to the logical order that I believe that you should follow when preparing your home to sell. You could however read the book in any order you wish.

The first few chapters concentrate on preparing your home for sale by de-cluttering, repairing, and staging your home. This will help with the showing of your home and create the most dramatic impact or impression your home can make.

The next few chapters help you understand how to market your home. There are chapters for pricing your home, taking pictures of your home, advertising and listing your home, and how to show your home to buyers. Many of the DIY aspects of selling your own home are found in these chapters and are what will save you on real estate commissions.

The last two chapters are dedicated to the offer and acceptance and contract, and title and closing. These chapters are there to ease your mind about selling your own home as I was scared at first to sell my own home. I thought to myself, Kevin, sure you can advertise your home for sale, take a bunch of pictures and all, but what are you going to do when someone makes an offer? You don't know what you are doing, you are not a professional. These chapters are what most of us want to know up front when we think of selling our homes ourselves. As I am still not an expert or professional in this area, I went to great lengths to ensure the accuracy of these chapters by consulting with a lawyer in the writing. I believe there is sufficient detail for you to understand what needs to be done, and will understand what professional services you will need to complete the transaction.

Step One: De-Clutter

Time involved: (2-6 weeks)

I believe it to be important to de-clutter as you prepare to sell your home. I estimate that this could take two to six weeks to accomplish, but could be shorter depending on your work schedule. Some people might think that de-cluttering is the same as cleaning your house, but as you read what I discuss here you'll see it's a little different. De-cluttering is about making the home visually appealing by minimizing the things you have and organizing what is left over. I don't mention cleaning your home in this book, as I consider it to be obvious that your home should be clean when preparing to show it for sale. While minimizing and rooting through your home de-cluttering, it would be a good idea to dust off and clean things as you go along.

When many people first purchase their homes, they either buy a home that suits their needs just right, or have bought a home sized a little too big. Either they feel cozy in the beginning or they feel that there is too much empty space. In both scenarios, we homeowners begin to accumulate things, and over time accumulate a great many things. This accumulated stuff begins to fill the house, filling every closet until there is no more empty space, there is no more cupboard space, the pantry is full, the porch is full, and then we start to fill the garage and attic with boxes. We buy shelving and storage systems for our spaces, and eventually we reach the point where we no longer have a place to put things.

When we reach the decision of selling our homes, many of us have a house full of clutter. We may even be selling our home so that we can buy a bigger home to accommodate all the stuff we have. It's likely that when we have come to the decision to sell our home, we have clutter to deal with, and we have a lot to do to prepare to sell our home.

One might ask, what is clutter, and how do I know if I have clutter? I have everything neat and organized, do I need to de-clutter? Why is it important to de-clutter? People aren't buying my things, they are buying the house. For the purpose of this book, and selling your home, we define clutter as anything in your home that does not serve the purpose of decorating your home for the purpose of displaying your home for sale. It's likely that even if you are organized, you still have some clutter when it comes to selling a home.

Just because everything you have has its place, or fits in a cabinet or closet, you still need to ask yourself, "Are the cabinets and closets full?" If the answer is yes, you may still need to de-clutter. It's important to de-clutter your home, because the impression a person gets by looking around in home will be a lasting impression in the mind of a buyer. How your home is decorated and displayed will drastically impact the perception in the buyer's mind.

It only takes a person a few seconds to determine whether or not to buy your home and you want your home looking its best. A person is going to spend their life's savings based on how they "feel" about the home and not about how much square footage there is, or whether there is new paint on the walls. People looking at your home are often interested or concerned about increasing their status, clarity of mind, efficiency, or achieving some desired mental or emotional effect that makes them feel better about themselves. It could be to your advantage to create the look that your home will increase a person's desired effect on their life. Having too much clutter can make this increase seem questionable. Nobody is thinking that they want to live in a dirtier, uglier, or more disorganized space than they currently have.

Now that I have you convinced that you need to de-clutter, let's jump into it and start the de-cluttering process. The first thing I recommend doing is putting four boxes together. Take a magic marker and label the first box "Trash," the second "Storage," the third "Garage Sale," and the fourth "Donation." You may substitute these labels for other purposes if you wish or add or subtract boxes. Then as you go through each room place these boxes close enough to get busy de-cluttering. Spend no more than ten seconds per item to decide whether to keep it or toss it. I personally filled five boxes to put in the trash, six boxes for a garage sale, three boxes for donation, and four boxes for storage. At the garage sale we raked in over $500 in two weekends, which was a nice bonus.

As you de-clutter areas of your home use this rule to know when you have de-cluttered enough. A given space should look 50% empty, whether it is a closet, cabinet, or drawer. You might be thinking to yourself that you have a lot of clutter and what are you to do with all the boxes? The solution is simple: rent a storage unit. I highly recommend renting one as soon as you start de-cluttering. Small storage units can be rented for less than $75 per month most of the time and you will need a place to put all of the things you de-cluttered that you are keeping and storing.

Below are areas and ideas for spaces that you want to de-clutter.

Kitchen & Dining Room Clutter:

The kitchen is a magnet for clutter. Almost everything ends up in the kitchen. We collect the mail, and we put the mail on the table or countertop. We carry our portable devices into the kitchen and have cell phone chargers plugged in next to the toaster. We put odd things in the kitchen from other areas of the house as a landing zone on the way to be put away. We almost all have a junk drawer with papers, pens, paper clips, drink straws, batteries, and all sorts of things making clutter. So what is important to de-clutter in the kitchen? Almost everything.

Starting with the most visible aspects, the countertop needs to be completely free of things. Put the coffee maker, toaster, dish rack, rice cooker, paper towel holder, wine bottles, and cookie jar into cabinets. If there is no room in the cabinet, then you need to reduce cabinet clutter.

Next, look at the top of the refrigerator and upper cabinets. Get rid of the cereal boxes on top of the fridge and put them in a cupboard or pantry. Get rid of decorations on top of your upper cabinets and put them in one of the boxes. Nothing should be visible above the fridge or cabinets. Then check the kitchen table, it should not have anything on it except a tablecloth, napkin holder, and salt and pepper shakers. You can put placemats out and other decorations but make sure they are decorations. If you have fine china, you may set the table with it. Do not have newspapers, magazines, bills, or other clutter on your table.

Finally, it's time to look in the cabinets and drawers to de-clutter the inside of them. Someone who is interested in your place will look inside the cabinets and drawers. They want to see the condition of the cabinets, and see how much space there is inside. They want to see how you have things organized and have an idea where they would put their own things. They want to know where the pots go, where you put your dishes, silverware, and cookware. A person wants to envision themselves living there and you want all the oddities out of your cabinets. As a rule of thumb your cabinets and drawers should look 50% empty. Keep your best kitchen gear in the kitchen, and find another place for the rest. If you have a cabinet full of plastic storage containers, get the containers out and put them in storage. Get anything that is old, broken, stained, or ugly out of the cabinets. Display your cabinets as if you are doing a photo shoot for a home and garden magazine, and make your cabinets look organized. If you have a food pantry, de-clutter it and empty up some space. Start with the old food items that you have not used in over three months and pack these up in your storage box. Plan to have your house sold within 30 days, and only have what you will eat in those 30 days in your pantry.

Living Room Clutter:

Many living rooms tend to collect clutter and sometimes are overly decorated. Some of us have collections of things on display in the living room. Others are movie buffs and have towers of movies. Some are eclectic, and have knickknacks on every surface. We have vacation mementos, shot glasses, collector spoons, coffee mugs, thimbles and other souvenirs in the living area. Most of this stuff needs to be taken out of the living room and stored.

Start with the most visible aspects. Clean out the entertainment area. Your TV and DVD player should be the only things on display in your entertainment system. The gaming console, games, controllers, and movies need to be stored away. This may seem difficult, because you may wonder, what am I going to do with my time off if everything is stored? The answer is that you will have plenty of things to do to keep busy to put your home on the market. Pretend that you have already sold your home and that you are slowly packing things away and are preparing to move. Once these things are packed they need to be put in a storage unit and not the garage. If you end up with a spare moment later on to relax, rent a movie on your pay per view or local movie kiosk.

Next, the collections we discussed above need to be put in a box and stored. Put away the vacation memories—pack-em and put-em storage. Another thing to pack away is all of the photos of you and your family. There should be no pictures of people anywhere in your house. Remember, people are trying to envision themselves in the space, and not you or other people. If you have children, all the children's toys need to be put in a designated toy room. Ensure that there is not a single item in the living room that is not a decoration. Knickknacks are not decorations! They are mementos or collections, and they need to be packed and stored.

Finally, consider some of the "lesser thought of" things. Many of us like to put a tablecloth or doily on every surface. They are personal touches, and should not be displayed unless they cover ugly furniture. The end tables should have a lamp on them, and that is it. The coffee table should have a centerpiece, like flowers or something that decorates the table. Bookshelves should be 50% empty of books and not have movies or games. Use bookends to keep the books in place. If you had family photos on the walls, and now you feel the walls are empty, place some framed art on the walls. Don't overdo it. Only place one art piece on the wall that matches the size and shape of the wall. Candleholders and wrought iron pieces fill up a wall and are attractive decorations. Look to second hand and charity stores for inexpensive temporary decorations.

Bathroom Clutter:

Bathrooms are clutter magnets like kitchens and are probably one of the hardest rooms to de-clutter in the entire house. The bathroom is one of the most heavily used rooms in the house, and has the tendency to attract things.

Starting with the most visible aspects, remove everything from the countertop. Nothing should be on the countertop except a fresh bar of soap, a folded washcloth, and a scented candle. Toothbrushes, toothpaste, hairbrush, hairspray, and makeup need to be put in a drawer, medicine cabinet, or in the storage area under the sink. The shower and bathtub should be completely empty except a fresh bar of soap on or in a soap dish. The shampoo, conditioner, razor, shaving cream, mirror, loofa, sponge, and the shower head caddy all need to be put away in a place other than the shower and bathtub. The bathroom should look like you have just stepped into a hotel, or a relaxing spa.

Next, get under the sink and into the cabinet. The cabinet should look half empty. Use storage containers to organize things. Have his and hers storage boxes for his stuff and her stuff. If your things cannot fit into the box, then put those things in storage. Keep things to a minimum in the cabinet. Your shampoo and other shower items can have their own basket and also be placed inside the cabinet. The medicine cabinet must also be de-cluttered and look spacious. Instead of having five bottles of perfume, reduce it to one. If you take medication, put them in a cloth zipper bag and place it in the sink cabinet. Nail clippers, combs, brushes, scissors, creams, lotions, and other items belong in a his or hers box and placed in the bathroom cabinet.

Finally, toiletry items need to be hidden away. Extra rolls of toilet paper can either be placed in the linen closet or under the sink, but don't make under the sink look cluttered by adding these things. The toilet plunger and toilet brush should be out of sight. Absolutely nothing should be on the toilet. Remember to think as if your house is already sold: you are moving, and you only have to live this way temporarily. Treat your bathroom as if you are living in a hotel room, and you only brought the minimum things you needed for your vacation with you. Keep bathroom decorations to a minimum. Most bathrooms only need one or two art pieces on the walls. Hang only one or two towels on the towel rack, and make sure that they are new, fluffy, white, or soft white. Don't display paisley printed towels or towels with fringes or tassels on them. As a last thought, the garbage can should remain empty at all times, with no trash bag in it.

Bedroom Clutter:

The bedroom is your personal sanctuary of the house. It is a personal space, and when we decide to sell our homes, it becomes open to the public and on display. You want the space to feel comfy, airy, clean, and relaxing. Many of us mistreat our bedrooms and have too many items in the bedroom. We have televisions, bookshelves, knickknacks, pictures, and a great many odds and ends stored in our bedrooms. Some use the bedroom for hiding things away that they don't want in the living room or kitchen. We store things in there because no one else normally ever goes into our bedrooms. It's time to roll up your sleeves and freshen up your sleeping areas.

Starting with the most visible aspects, clean off the dressers and nightstands. Nothing should be on these surfaces except decorative items. The dresser should have a centerpiece decoration. Flowers or scented candles are attractive decorations that can be used as the center piece. Jewelry boxes should be packed and stored. Radios and televisions need to be put in storage. The nightstand should only have a lamp and an alarm clock—no doily.

The fun part of de-cluttering the bedroom is that you don't have to clean out the dressers. No one should be looking inside your dressers as they don't come with the house. You can cram whatever you want into the dressers and nightstands and keep all the clutter you want in them.

Next, when it comes to the closet, move all your clothes to one side to open up the space and ensure that you are only using half of the space or less. Boxes, shoes, purses, bags, suitcases, and umbrellas need to comply with our de-cluttering rules, and things that exceed the threshold need to be stored.

Finally, ensure that the bed does not have excess items on it. You should have a nice bedspread with coordinating pillow shams. There should be no teddy bears, embroidered pillows or other items on the bed. Make sure that the laundry basket is in the laundry room, or in the closet. If you store the laundry basket in the closet make sure it is not making the closet look cluttered. There should be nothing on the floor in the bedroom other than furniture. The same applies to children's rooms: toys need to be picked up and put in the toy box. If the toy box cannot fit all the toys, then pack excess toys and store them.

Garage Clutter:

Cleaning out the garage and de-cluttering it can be a monstrous task. Many things get dumped in the garage, as they may not have a space in your home. People store boxes upon boxes in the garage. Most likely it is filled with sports equipment, bicycles, Christmas decorations, old clothes, seasonal items, beach gear, tools, and gardening equipment. However, cleaning out the clutter of the garage can be easy if you follow these steps.

Starting with the most visible aspects, consider putting most of the things in your garage in storage. If you already have things in the garage marked for garage sale, hold on to the boxes for your upcoming garage sale. If you have a box for donating, combine it with the things you accumulated from the above processes and bring them all to the donation center. The trick is to get as many things out of sight as is humanly possible. If you have a storage shelf system, make sure that everything on that system is put in a box and looks neat. If you have cabinets in the garage, organize them, fitting things where you can. It is not so important in this step that the cabinets are 50% empty in the garage. Some storage is expected. The important aspect is that the garage looks clean and mostly empty.

Next, consider putting bicycles and excess sports equipment in storage. Keep most things off the floor. Ensure that if your garage can accommodate two cars that it actually has the room to store two cars without clutter being in the way. Ensure that tools are put away, preferably out of sight, and garden tools are either hung on the wall, organized, or stored away. Don't have a corner of the garage with a bunch of rakes and shovels tucked into it.

Finally, make sure that the garage is presentable, like the rest of your home is after de-cluttering. Carefully choose what really needs to stay in the garage. You might have a lot of boxes stored away in the garage at this point from de-cluttering other areas of the house. Take these boxes to your rented storage unit and you will be one step closer to selling your home.

Use the companion website at http://www.realestate-forsalebyowner.com to find checklists that are printable for your de-cluttering process.

Step Two: Repair

Time Involved: (1-3 weeks)

After having lived in your home for a period of time, one of two scenarios will be the case. Either you kept up on all the maintenance or you have neglected the maintenance. Home maintenance means that all the expected items that should be cared for while living in your home are currently in good condition. This involves caulking, and the proper type of caulking for the application. It means that plumbing and fixtures are in good working order, clean and free of rust and stains. It means that the furnace and furnace filter are clean. It means that flooring is well taken care of, free of stains, burns, and scratches. The roof should have longevity. Finally, it means that your home is in good working order and that no significant repairs are needed.

It is important to do all the minor repairs that you are capable of doing yourself before showing your home for the first time. When people come to look at your home, they are also doing a visual inspection of any noticeable repairs that may be needed. Most people want to buy a "turnkey" property, which means that no maintenance or repairs are required upon move in. Potential buyers will look at the caulking around windows, the caulking in the bathrooms, they will look under sinks for leaks, and they will look for anything that is visually noticeable. Don't just offer your home for sale at a discount: fix these items and offer it for sale at a premium.

Below is an explanation of some of the easiest repairs you can do yourself or things you definitely want to repair before showing your home or taking pictures for advertising.

Caulking:

There are three main types of caulking on the market. The first type of caulking is painting and trim caulking. Next, there is indoor/outdoor caulking. Finally there is kitchen and bathroom caulking. Make sure that the type of caulking that you are using matches the application. I recommend buying a painter's multipurpose tool. This one tool will strip old caulking and clean your paint rollers. They are actually quite handy for many applications, especially for stripping caulking. I do not recommend using a razor blade or utility knife for stripping caulking. It will make the job ten times more difficult. When applying the caulking (this applies to all caulking applications) make sure that you cut the caulking tube short of the ⅛" line. The thinner the bead of caulking the easier it is to get a sharp and clean look. You will need a thin wire or something long, skinny and sharp to puncture the seal of the caulking. Working with a thin bead of caulking is much easier and less messy. If you need extra caulking for a wide space, just caulk over it multiple times until the space is filled. Once the space is filled, dip your finger in water and wipe it over the bead of caulk to smooth it out.

Many people seem to overlook the effect of properly caulked trim. Caulked trim looks great, and helps in achieving a clean and crisp look. If your trim is missing caulk, or the caulk is dried and shriveled, clean the old caulk off with the multipurpose painter's tool and re-caulk the trim. Trim that is pulled away from the wall is an eyesore, and will attract attention. I recommend that you re-caulk these areas.

When it comes to windows and doors, experienced home buyers will inspect the caulking of the windows and doors. Don't underestimate the fact that experienced buyers will notice the little details. Cracked caulking around windows and doors spells trouble in the mind of prospective buyers. Plus, it just looks better that windows and doors have fresh caulking. Make sure that you buy indoor/outdoor caulking for this application.

When it comes to kitchens and bathrooms, silicone caulking is the only solution. Luckily you won't need a lot of it. Silicone caulking tends to be the hardest to strip away, so be prepared to use some elbow grease to get it loose. By the same token, silicone caulking tends to last the longest (15 years), so it won't be necessary to replace if you only lived in a new home for only a few years.

One last thought about caulking: although you might believe it necessary, do not caulk around your toilets! This is one of the most common mistakes people make. You don't want caulking all the way around toilets, because if the toilet wax seal that joins the toilet to the plumbing fails, then you will never know. All of the rotting sewage will be on your floor under your toilet, and it will inevitably lead to a rotten floor and more damage than you want to deal with. If you must caulk around the toilet, only caulk the front half, and do not caulk the rear of the toilet.

Plumbing and Fixtures:

It is absolutely necessary that there be no leaks or drips under any sink in your home. The good news is that you don't need to call a plumber to fix most leaks or drips. There are only two sources of leaks or drips, and these are the water supply or the drain. Both the water supply and drain are easy to repair when it comes to leaks or drips.

For the water supply there is normally a flexible hose that connects from the shut off valve to the copper pipes of the faucet. At either end of this hose there can be leaks. With a crescent wrench, tighten the connection that drips a ¼ turn. Then wipe the connection clean of water, and place a paper towel under the area of the connection and wait to see if the drip stops. If you find more dripping, repeat this process until the drip stops.

For the drain there are typically only three pipe fittings with three connections to hand tighten. First there is a drain pipe connecting to the sink, which is almost never the source of a leak. Second, there is a pipe that slips onto the first pipe and is fastened in place with a slip washer and a nut. You will see that the pipe is flanged to slip onto the first pipe and the pipe itself is a "U" shape, which is known as the drain trap (P-Trap). If you see a leak or drip where the first pipe connects to the drain trap, then hand tighten the nut, but normally the pipes wont leak here. When tightening any of the drain pipes under the sink make sure to only hand tighten the pipe nuts; normally, no tools are required. If you have metal drain pipes and they are rusted together, you might need a tool to loosen or tighten the pipe nut. But most of the time metal drain pipes only need hand tightening. Third, there is a pipe that connects to the trap called the trap arm. This pipe has a curved lip on it to create a seal with the trap. This is a spot where you will commonly find leaks. Hand tighten this nut firmly into place to stop leaks or drips. Finally, the other end of the trap arm should go directly into the fixed rigid plumbing, going into the wall. Where the trap arm connects to the rigid plumbing is a common area for leaks and drips. The trap arm is fastened to the rigid plumbing with a slip washer and pipe nut. If you find a leak or drip here, tighten the pipe nut firmly into place.

Furnace:

The furnace is fairly easy to do some do-it-yourself cleaning. Some simple cleaning to the furnace will save you some money from having to pay someone to do it. I only write about it here because it is an easy thing to do and will save you money. A home inspector will almost always point out a dirty furnace and the buyer will ask to have it serviced. A furnace cleaning normally costs $60-$90, yet the job is very easy. For the process described below, which is for a typical gas furnace, the things you need are simply a vacuum cleaner, rag, cleaning spray, canned air, and a paintbrush.

Disclaimer: cleaning your furnace yourself is not the same or a substitute for having your furnace inspected or serviced by a qualified technician.

Start by ensuring that the power to the furnace is off. There is normally a light switch on or next to the furnace that controls the electrical elements of the furnace. Don't trust the thermostat for simply turning off the furnace. If you are uncertain whether the furnace is off, consult the product documentation or hire a technician.

Next, remove the furnace panels on the front. They will most likely slide upward for removal. Place these panels aside and locate the furnace filter. Remove and inspect the filter; if it looks dirty or is full of dust, replace it. It generally is a good practice to replace the filters every 3 months during heating season. Then visually inspect the furnace blower fan, which is a circular looking squirrel cage. Is the squirrel cage dirty or full of dust? If so, make a mental note for now, and clean it while cleaning other parts of the furnace.

Next, begin cleaning the areas that were covered by the panels. Use the paintbrush to loosen the dust on circuit panels and wires. Use the canned air to blow off dust in hard to reach areas, or dust that is stubborn. Use the vacuum cleaner hose attachment to vacuum up any loose dust. Do the same for the squirrel cage, but make certain that the furnace is off. Use the cleaning rag dampened with cleaning solution to wipe down metal surfaces. When finished the furnace should have a general clean look.

Check with the manufacturer's documentation on how often your furnace should be inspected or serviced. During the inspection or servicing the furnace technician should check the combustion chamber flame to determine the overall condition of the furnace. If something is wrong at the time of servicing, you may need to have them do the necessary repairs to ensure proper operation.

Flooring:

Ensure that your flooring is in the best condition that it can be before showing your home. The flooring should be clean, vacuumed, and possibly shampooed before showing. I know that your flooring may not be perfect after living in the home for a number of years, but it's important to do what you can.

For carpeted floors, stain treat areas that have stains or heavy traffic. It might be necessary for you to hire a professional carpet cleaner if your carpets are heavily soiled or have a lot of stains. Having your carpets professionally cleaned is recommended and is prudent before showing your home. They can sometimes get persistent stains out of carpet that you might not be able to with a home carpet shampoo system, because the carpet cleaner typically uses much hotter water to get your carpets clean. Resources for professional carpet cleaning services can be found on my website.

For tile floors, normally you should be able to clean them yourself, but if you have a lot of stained grout, consider having the carpet cleaner clean your tile. Make sure that you call in advance and ask if they also clean tile. Some do clean tile and they do an excellent job, restoring the grout to new looking.

For hardwood floors I recommend that you spend time scrubbing the floors clean and waxing them. If your hardwood has some scratches, I would personally let it ride. If your hardwood is heavily scratched, you could consider hiring a professional to resurface your hardwood, but in most cases, I believe this to be unnecessary, and that if the new owner wants to resurface the floors they will do it at their own expense. The fact that you have hardwood is a bonus, and most people have a high tolerance for scratches.

Good Working Order:

The other features of your home should also be in good working order. Your doors, windows, blinds, and garage door should be in good working order. They should close properly, they should not stick, and should operate normally.

These are smaller annoyances that may or may not need attention. However, if they can be corrected inexpensively, they could be included in your list of things to do. They will possibly show up in the home inspection, and may be requested to be corrected by the buyer anyway. Your concentration should mainly focus on what a typical buyer might find in the showing. You want the showing to go off without a hitch. Then after the showing you can negotiate with the buyer on what you must fix.

Use the companion website at http://www.realestate-forsalebyowner.com to find do-it-yourself repair articles for repairing your home.

Step Three: Staging

Time Involved: (1-3 weeks)

Staging is a very important step in preparing your home for sale. Most real estate agents agree that a staged home sells faster and for a higher price than a home that is not staged.

Staging is a difficult thing to write about in a single chapter of a book, as staging itself is something of an art, and somewhat about personal taste. For simplicity, I will discuss some of the basics, and try to leave the reader with an understanding what a well-staged home looks like.

I strongly advise hiring a consultant to help in the staging of your home. Resources for staging can be found on the companion website. A consultation can be as simple as single consultation, where they offer suggestions on how to improve your staging for a small consultation fee of normally about $75. Otherwise you can hire them to do the bulk of the work for additional fees. While some people are good at staging their home themselves, others may not be able to see their home's full potential. If you follow the suggestions in this book, then it is likely you will save enough money on commissions to pay for some minimal services like hiring a professional stager for a consultation. The points below are simple suggestions to give you a flavor of what staging might look like.

If you followed the recommendations in chapter one on de-cluttering then the staging process will be much easier. Staging is just as much about de-cluttering as it is about making your spaces look great. This point can't be emphasized enough: de-cluttering is 75% of the work involved in staging. If your home is not de-cluttered staging won't have the desired impact if your home is bursting stuff out of every closet. If you have already de-cluttered at this point, then staging will be more about re-organizing, rearranging, and decorating your home for best impact.

Think of the staging process as if you are taking a picture of the rooms of your home for a popular magazine. You want the rooms of your home to look fresh, clean, organized and lived in all at the same time. Imagine, if you will, the homes featured in magazines: there is always one thing that was carefully set out of place to catch your eye's attention. That something is always something that is inviting and that draws your attention. For example, envision an advertisement about a grocery store, and the advertisement features a person walking out of the front of the store with a paper shopping bag. Of course the person will be smiling, and the bag will feature the store's name. The small thing that will likely draw your attention is what is in the bag, or rather what is sticking out of the top of the paper bag, which was meticulously placed in the bag only to grab your attention. Likely there will be a loaf of crusty French bread sticking out of the top, along with a box of spaghetti noodles, and celery. This gives you the impression of freshness, wholesomeness, and heartiness. It might make you think that it's been a while since you had spaghetti and may tempt you to rush out the door to go buy the ingredients.

This is what the essence of staging is: it's about leaving some things out of place to create wonder, imagination, and the feeling of living there. The remaining part of this chapter is divided into the rooms that you will want to ensure are staged well, and some ideas for creating interest.

Kitchen:

The kitchen should be one of the most inviting places in your home. It should feel clean, fresh, homey, and create a sense of activity and purpose. The kitchen should be brightly lit with harder solid color tones and have some contrasting colors to make highlights stand out. Textures should be cold and hard and look professional. People want to feel as though they are celebrity chefs in their kitchens, so pay attention to colors and textures. The kitchen is the most important room of the house to get staging right, as the kitchen alone can sell the house.

The kitchen is an easy room of the house for staging. At this point it should be clear that the kitchen should be de-cluttered and free of anything floating around on the counters. The dishes and all small appliances should be hidden and put away in the cabinets before you worry about how it should be decorated.

Simplicity is key for the kitchen. The walls should be minimally decorated. Possibly there should be only a clock as a decoration on the wall of the kitchen. For larger kitchens, one or two other wall decorations will surely suffice. The fewer things you have for decorations, the easier it is to coordinate the look. The decorations should not be gimmicky or convey your highly personal tastes. Magnets on the refrigerator do not count as decorations and you should remove all of them.

Rather than focusing on the walls, focus more on what is in the kitchen, like the things you did not put away from the de-clutter process. Are these things neat, clean, and modern? Do they coordinate well? Are you are keeping to a minimum of things on the counter? Do these things match in color, quality, and material? If not, consider sticking to one theme and hiding the rest.

Consider adding a touch of flare in your kitchen by adding solid colored kitchen towels. Drape one on the sink, partly in the sink and partly outside. It will create the look that you may have just completed washing and drying the dishes. It gives the sense of the home being lived in. Drape another over the stove handle. Have the oven mittens match the towels. Have a luxurious cooking vessel on the stove—possibly Le Creuset—and a matching spoon at the side. Create the look that you are about ready to cook dinner.

Ensure that the kitchen smells clean. Make sure to take out the garbage every day, and fight against offensive odors. Use an air freshener that smells bright, like citrus or floral. If you have a window in the kitchen, keep it open as much as possible to invite fresh air in.

Definitely think about what food to leave out on the counter. Many people will leave out fresh baked cookies, but this is not always practical and somewhat unoriginal. A good way to make an impression is to buy a whole cake from a restaurant or bakery that features a nice gift box. Prominently displaying the cake can hint at social status. Another idea is to buy some food from a prominent store like Whole Foods, and leave the grocery bag on the counter by the stove. Display it as was described above. Definitely have things peering out the top of the bag. Another common approach is to display a bowl of fresh fruit on the counter, which is a nice accompanying item that signifies health.

Dining Room:

The dining room is a room for conversation, family time, and togetherness. The dining room should feel luxurious, sophisticated, warm, and bold. You want to create the feeling of comfort and pride. It should invite people to want to stay for lengthy amounts of time for conversations after a meal. It should have medium to low lighting to create a feeling of warmth.

Staging a dining room is all about making the space work. If you have de-cluttered as described above, then there won't be much work involved in the dining room. Arranging the dining room should be fairly simple at this point. Do a self-assessment of the dining room. Does it look too full? Does it look cluttered? The space should look mostly empty. The table should be centered in the room with the chairs pushed in to the edge of the table and you should be able to walk around the dining room table without squeezing between things and sucking in your gut.

If the dining room looks too full consider removing things and putting them in storage. This could be a hutch or a buffet table that takes up too much space. Use your best judgment on this. Can you comfortably sit around the dining room table without dinging the chairs on the hutch or buffet table? If so, you're good; if not, remove the hutch or buffet table. It's natural to be attached to your own things, and think that they really add to your style. But take the common sense approach. Buyers want to see how "their" things will fit your home, not "your" things. Open space speaks loudly for your home, and are key to making your home look appealing.

Minimally decorate the walls with a single painting and complementing candleholders. Avoid family pictures and personal touches. Don't fret over bare walls. You want to focus buyers' attention on a few sophisticated things. Cluttered walls draw attention to the wrong things in your home.

Create interest in the dining room by setting the table for two at opposing ends of the table. Set the table as if you are about to have a romantic dinner with your loved one. On the center of the table have a bouquet of flowers and possibly a bottle of champagne.

However, keep it simple and don't overdo with unnecessary candlesticks, or napkin holders.

Living Room:

The living room is a multipurpose room that should feel relaxing, inviting, entertaining, tranquil, and soothing all at the same time. It should feel warm, cozy, and lively. These are contrasting ideas that define the living space. People spend free time in the living room and it needs to suit multiple purposes. People watch television, read, nap, play games, and converse in the living room. For this reason the living room needs to appeal to multiple sensations.

If you haven't already done so, put the personal photos of your family in storage. Replace the family photos with paintings or art work. This will make the space feel more neutral and neutrality is what you want to appeal to the various uses of the living room. Stick to neutral colors to accent your living room. Colors such as beige, cream, light browns, and other soft colors. Use these colors to accent any bold colors you may already have in the living room.

Then concentrate on minimizing the space. Do you really need a couch, loveseat, and two chairs in the living room? If your living room feels cramped put some of the items in storage. Consider putting the loveseat in storage and keeping the couch and two chairs or what works best for the space. You can play with the arrangement to see what is most appealing to you.

Chances are your buyers will prefer an open space compared to a cramped feeling.

You should be able to walk through the living room into the next room without hurdling over or edging around things. Don't allow yourself to be attached to your things. Most people tend to maximize the amount of things they can put in a living room, based on what they have as furniture. Don't be afraid to sell the sectional couch you have and buy a single three cushion couch. The three cushion couch will open up the room tremendously compared to the sectional. Don't get me wrong, sectionals can work in some spaces, but often they take up too much space and can make your living room look small.

Create interest by making the living room feel lived in. A comfy knitted blanket on the sofa can set a mood for relaxation and taking a nap. Have a book or magazine on the coffee table. These things give the buyer the perception that you and your family enjoy the space, which translates to them enjoying it too.

Bathrooms:

The bathroom is just as important to stage as any other room of the house. The bathroom should feel clean and refreshing. The aim of staging a bathroom should make it feel like you just stepped into a full service spa.

To create the spa-like look, start with minimizing everything in the bathroom. Have only a single decoration on the wall. Neatly hang a fresh, fluffy, folded, white towel on the towel rack. Have the shower curtain open, so that you can see inside the shower area and open up the space. Have a rolled towel placed on the edge of the tub. If your bathroom has the space, put either a bamboo or orchid plant on the counter. Keep the counter to very few items other than a new fresh bar of soap in the soap dish.

Place a folded washcloth on the edge of the sink, partly draped into the sink. This makes the bathroom look like it is ready for use. Place a luxurious perfume or cologne on the counter that can hint at sophistication. Avoid keeping the toothbrush, hairbrush, and other items on the counter as indicated in the de-cluttering chapter. These other things will look like clutter. Put those things in the medicine cabinet or under the sink in the cabinet. If you don't have a cabinet then keep those things in a toiletry bag in the closet.

Bedrooms:

The bedrooms should feel fresh, comfortable, relaxing, and stress free for resting. They should be dimly lit with soft color tones. People want to feel that they will have peace and tranquility in the bedroom.

To accomplish this, be careful with color choices and textures. Pastel colors work well for bedding pillows and decoration. Steer away from solid bold colors. Colors that are too bright will make the room feel active and lively. Colors that are too dark will make the room feel despairing and cold. Regarding textures, choose softer elements like light colored woods, fabrics, and materials. Steer away from metals or use them sparingly. Create a clean smell in this area by keeping your linens and bedding clean by freshly washing regularly. Buy some scented candles with a clean smell, and light them especially before a showing if you have an advance notice. Also get matching plug-in air fresheners and leave them plugged in constantly. A bottle of Febreze may be necessary if you have a persistent unpleasant odor in the room.

Arrange furniture in the bedroom to maximize free movement. Do this by placing the bed in the middle of the wall on the side of the room opposite the door and placing dressers and nightstands where they do not create an obstacle while walking through the bedroom. People will likely walk from the bedroom door to the closet and master bath. Make pathways to get to these areas with ease. Avoid placing the bed in the corner with walls touching the bed on two sides. The idea is to open up the space and making it appear that there is plenty of room to arrange the room in other ways. If necessary, definitely consider downsizing the bed from a king to a queen, if you are short on space.

Create interest by having the bed made, but simply have the sheets and covers on one side of the bed turned down, like it is ready for going to sleep. Leave an interesting book—possibly a romance novel—on the night stand. This will help potential buyers envision themselves sleeping there—along with other thoughts. Another trick is to leave a department store shopping bag on the dresser. Pick something that is priced appropriately for the expected buyer's income. The prospective buyers won't feel that your home is just on display, and it might help them envision their ideal life in your home. Do this will help them remember your home when they get around to comparing their options.

Use the companion website at http://www.realestate-forsalebyowner.com to find additional resources on staging your home.

Step Four: Price

Time Involved: (1 week or less)

With your home de-cluttered, repaired, and staged you are now ready to set your selling price. Setting the price to sell your home can be nerve wracking. Most of us want to maximize the amount of money we can earn on the sale of our home and pricing your home correctly can make the difference of thousands of dollars. As a rule of thumb a home is priced correctly if you have approximately 3-5 showings a week, and in the course of a month, you should have an offer.

If you are not making three showings a week then you might consider dropping your price after the second week. Depending on your area you will want to consider dropping the price by 5%-10% to increase your number of showings significantly. At this new set point restart your count on the number of showings to see if the price change makes a difference.

If you are having more than three to five showings a week, or even as many per day, then your price could be too low and you could be missing out on some profits. In this case, you can do one of two things. Either increase the advertised price, or keep the price and hope for multiple offers at the same time. In the latter case wait as long as possible to accept an offer. Waiting the maximum amount of time will allow for the possibility to have two offers and create a bidding war among the buyers, and then stand the chance of getting your full price or more.

The next few topics are about how you might go about setting your sale price.

Hire an Appraiser:

A very good way to accurately price your home is to hire your own appraiser to appraise your home. The benefits are that you can rest comfortably knowing that the price you set on your home is not too high, or too low. An accurate and fair price will help sell the home faster. Too low a price on your home could cause some people to think that there is something wrong with the place. Too high a price will also turn some people away as some may believe that home is overpriced and won't appraise for the asking price.

It is a common practice for real estate agents to ask for the comps on the home to help their clients better judge the value of the home. Your appraisal report will have a number comps in it. It can be used as a tool to help you sell the house. One strategy is to have the appraisal report available for viewing during your showings. Interested buyers that make an offer are more likely to make offers close to the appraisal, without trying to lowball their offer. A professional appraisal will typically only cost between $150 and $225. This is a small cost and an item you should plan to hire a professional, and there are many benefits of having an appraisal done even if you were to hire a real estate agent.

Do Your Own CMA:

One might also decide to do their own Comparative Market Analysis (CMA). Most real estate agents know this process very well and there is normally a service included when you agree to pay traditional commissions to a real estate agent. The CMA process is very similar to what a paid appraiser does, except appraisers are licensed to appraise your home.

The CMA is another good DIY task that you should do in the course of selling your home. For most people, following the simple procedures I outline below will land you relatively close to your home's value. But if you are not a professional or a real estate agent without experience of appraising homes, expect that you could be off on your own home evaluation by as much as 10%-20 %. You must exercise caution when setting the price of your home. However, it's still recommended to do a DIY appraisal of your home, as this can be helpful in understanding an actual paid appraisal if you hired one. Additionally, if you hire an appraiser then you can give them the comparable homes you chose, and ask them to consider them in their report.

The CMA process I describe involves three steps. Find three to five homes that are very similar to your home for each of the following: homes that are for sale, homes that are under contract, and homes that have been sold in the last 0 to 6 months. Sometimes it is difficult to find homes that are similar to yours, as your home might have unique features. The trick is to find homes that match features and square footage as closely as possible.

The goal in doing your own CMA is to compare your home with homes that are within one square mile. If your home is in a subdivision, try to only use homes that are the same as yours in your subdivision and try to compare your home to homes that were built by the same builder. This will likely result in you making fewer errors when trying to price your home.

There are a few ways to collect this information. One way is to use your local real estate listing service that the real estate agents in your local area use. Search for homes that are for sale in your area, within a mile, with the same features, bedrooms, baths, square footage. Sometimes these listing services will also list the homes that are currently under contract and ones that recently sold. However, the searching capabilities for individual use on those listing services is limited, and only members of their real estate listing service can do advanced searches for under contract and homes sold. Another resource to use is Zillow. On Zillow you can search for homes for sale and homes recently sold, but lacks the feature for homes under contract. Another disadvantage is that Zillow's database might not be as complete as the real estate listing service that real estate agents use. Finally there is one last resource to check for homes sold, and that is your county clerk's database on recent homes that were sold in your area.

Some counties have this information available on a web page, so be sure to check this as it is very reliable if it exists.

Once you have done so, collect the above listing of properties to the best of your ability. Don't worry if you fall short on the number of properties, just do your best. Once in hand, then you need to start comparing the properties to your property. Arbitrarily, you need to try and articulate the differences between the properties and assign value to these differences.

For instance, your home might have granite countertops, and the home you compare to might not. Then you would want to adjust the value of your home to be slightly higher than the home without. However, don't expect to increase the value of your home by a large margin over countertops. Don't expect to get a full value difference for the countertops. Home valuations don't work that way, even though it would seem that it should.

There are many factors that go into the value of your home, and it's the aggregate of these factors that determine the price. It's a mistake to think that you added $10,000 in value to your home because it's the price you paid when you upgraded your home. This methodology won't work and it will be a mistake if you consider your home upgrades in this way.

Your home upgrades typically won't command a high return on your dollar. Be extremely conservative on these differences between your home and the comparable homes. These differences in your home is what the appraiser is best at judging, and is why I advocate their use. However, I feel compelled to give the reader some factor to use for planning purposes. Strictly arbitrarily, one should not want to use more than 50% of the cost of those granite countertops when adjusting one's home value to a comparable one. However, I could be wrong, I am not an appraiser and every home has unique considerations that factor into the total price.

Use Zillow:

One consideration to use when pricing your home is to use Zillow's website at http://www.zillow.com/. The web service assigns a value to every home with what they call the Zestimate. This feature of Zillow is very good for helping you determining the value of your home. There are a few things that you need to know about Zillow before just blindly using Zillow's Zestimate.

First know that Zillow's accuracy depends on your home's facts, and the facts need to be correct in their database. Make sure that when you log into Zillow that you claim ownership of your home. When you do this Zillow allows you to make some edits about your home. The information in your home profile are some of the things Zillow's algorithm uses to determine your home's value. So ensure that you log in and update your home facts— http://www.zillow.com/zestimate/.

Next, know that Zillow's Zestimate has various accuracy rates based on a number of factors. It could be as accurate as 5% of your home's value, or it could be less accurate at 20%. The factors for accuracy vary wildly based on city, age of home, type of home, and other factors. Zillow claims that the Zestimate should only be used as a starting point. In my personal experience I listed my home 10% above the Zestimate, and settled on a selling price that was 5% above the Zestimate.

If you decide to use Zillow for pricing your home, use caution. Ensure that you do some side homework and compare your property to others as a normal real estate agent would by doing a CMA or hiring an appraiser with the money you are saving by reading this book.

Tax Appraisal:

Finally, consider using your tax appraisal as a basis for determining your home value. Your tax appraisal should be fairly close to your home value and is a good resource to consider when setting your home's price. However, there are some reasons that the appraisal could be a little off from the market value and you will want to know about these additional considerations.

Your tax appraisal likely won't factor in your granite countertops and other upgrades to your home that did not require permits. It likely won't factor in landscaping and many other upgrades. So one must use some caution when using the tax appraisal and make necessary adjustments for these factors.

Also consider that the tax appraisal is only updated annually, and its accuracy will depend on how long ago the appraisal was updated. If the appraisal was updated 10 months ago, and the price of real estate has fluctuated since the appraisal, you will need to adjust for that.

Check with your county appraiser's office to see how accurately they appraise homes. Some offices will state that they appraise homes within certain accuracy guidelines for tax purposes. For instance, your property tax appraisal might only reflect a home's value according to the value of the home the year prior. If this is the case, then you want to make necessary adjustments. Call your county appraiser or check their website for this information, it can be very helpful in determining the value of your home.

Finally, you can use your county appraiser's website for obtaining the tax appraisal of the homes close to you, and this could be additional supporting information in determining the price of your home.

Use the companion website at http://www.realestate-forsalebyowner.com to find additional resources on pricing your home.

Step Five: Pictures

Time Involved: (1 week or less)

Hire a Real Estate Photographer:

The photographs of your home are as important as any of the other processes mentioned above. They are the greeting and invitation that inspire people to come see your home in person. By hiring a real estate photographer you are ensuring that your photos are professional, appealing, and attractive.

Most people probably have seen pictures of houses or apartments where the photograph is a picture of a corner of a room. This is because the pictures weren't taken professionally and were taken with a personal point-and-shoot camera. These cameras are typically zoomed into a particular fixed number of feet that causes the camera to miss the first 5 feet to the left and right of the photographer. Photographers have professional cameras, and are able to compensate for zoom factors, lighting, and other factors that can make your photos more appealing. Photographers typically have numerous lenses for their cameras that perform specialized functions. For most pictures in your home the photographer will typically use a wide angle lens. This lens ensures that pictures won't be zoomed into the corner of a room. For extra tight spaces they will use a fisheye lens, which distorts the look of the room, but captures much more to the left and right of the photographer.

Hiring a photographer will typically cost $75 to $100 for about an hour's worth of picture taking and the digital copies of the photos. During the picture taking, you will want to be personally involved to ensure that there aren't any distractions in the photos like dirty laundry, dish rags, or things that don't belong in the photo. Be prepared to move things around to get rid of these distractions as the photographer takes pictures. One advantage of using a photographer is that they are trained to judge the lighting of rooms and will typically have flash devices that will compensate for dark or shadowy corners. This helps ensure that the lighting in the photos is appropriate and appealing.

Take Your Own Photos:

Some people might feel comfortable with taking their own photos as they might have their own professional camera equipment. Possibly, if you know of someone who has professional equipment, then you might be able to get their assistance in photographing your home. If you choose to take your own photos, then ensure that you take the photos with a quality camera.

One trick that can help you with taking pictures of tight spaces is to use a smartphone that has panning capability. This allows the user to take a continuous photo while pivoting the camera from left to right for a panoramic shot to reveal more of the area.

Ensure that areas of the home that you take pictures of are well lit. It's best to take pictures on brighter days during the middle of the day. That way the light from outside will help make the photos look brighter and more natural. Turn on all of the lights in a room when photographing a room, and if it is necessary, you might want to consider increasing the amount of light with lamps.

Take Your Own Video:

One might also decide to take one's own video recording of their home. Video recordings of the home are becoming increasingly popular. A video helps potential buyers envision the look and feel of the home. It puts the pictures in perspective and helps the buyer understand the layout of your home.

Just about any video recording device will suffice for taking a video of your home. However, there are a few things that you should keep in mind. First, make sure your house is perfectly staged throughout the entire house. Next, make sure you turn on all the lights in the house in advance. Finally make sure you go through your home in a fairly quick manner recording the entire home in about 5 minutes. You want to keep the video short as possible to conserve the resulting file size. It is not necessary to record your home in full HD. A smaller format like 800 x 600 is plenty.

Use YouTube to upload your file to the internet. Once uploaded, you can copy the short link to your video for putting it on Zillow, Craigslist, and Facebook.

Use the companion website at http://www.realestate-forsalebyowner.com to find additional resources about photographing your home.

Step Six: Advertise

Time Involved: (1-2 weeks)

Congratulations! If you followed the steps recommended above, then you are ready to put your home on the market and start showing your home. It is both an exciting and frightening time to have your home on the market. If you are new to the process of selling your own home, then you probably have a great many questions at this stage of the game. This stage tends to be a little scary for some, as one might be entering into uncharted waters. The goal of this book is to help make the reader feel at ease with selling their own home, so keep reading: you are a little over halfway there to having peace of mind.

Below are some of the methods that you should consider when actively marketing your home. Pick and choose which methods you want to use. The methods will have varying results based on your area. I have assigned a percentage to each category on what I believe are typical results for generating leads. These percentages however are not scientific and there was no survey taken to ensure the accuracy, so take the percentages with a grain of salt. Consider the percentages as a starting point on where to place your effort. These percentages represent what my results were in my experience of selling my home.

Try to think of advertising as a numbers game. The more methods you use, the more people you reach out to, which results in more showings and a faster sale. I personally used most all the methods that I discuss below.

Listing Service:

In my experience I received 60% of my leads from my local real estate listing service. The reader will have to research what the local listing service is in their market. Commonly this service might go by the letter acronym MLS®, which is a registered trademark. When I was selling my home I paid for this type of listing service, but at the time I did not know clearly what I was buying. I paid nearly $400 for a six month listing on my local listing service. What I did not know is that connected with this payment were additional services provided to me by the real estate agent.

Inadvertently I paid for extra services with the purchase of the listing. It turned out to be a pleasant surprise that I now had a real estate agent to work with. To my great pleasure my agent gave me many of the same services that one might expect paying for a commissioned agent. Once I signed him on he was my guide for the duration of my listing and all the way through closing. As my guide, he coached me on all the tasks I needed to accomplish and walked me through how to handle calls and showings. Some of the things not to expect with this service are CMA, staging, picture taking, showing your home, and having open houses. These remain your DIY tasks. However there are some additional things they do for you that at first I did not expect. Once I got an offer on my place my agent consulted with me on the offer and walked me through the entire offer and acceptance, and contract details all the way up to closing.

As it turns out with these listing services there are certain requirements for listing your home on these services that can vary based on your state laws or local area norms. In my area, there was a requirement to be a real estate agent to become a member of the listing service and to advertise properties on this service. So in my case the payment for the listing service was an actual flat-fee payment for a qualified real estate agent to list my home on the service.

Most people are aware of their local real estate listing service, it is normally most popular and centralized database in their area. These are a very powerful resource for listing homes for sale and the service is normally a membership based service for real estate companies and professionals. These listing services are commonly associated with the realtors.com® website, which is another very powerful resource for advertising your home. When listed on these services you can be assured that the majority of all people contacting you will be from this service offering.

These services are typically very comprehensive and very detailed about all your home facts like the number of bedrooms, bathrooms, living rooms, and kitchens and their sizes. It will list many of the features of your home, like the type of flooring, type of roof, water heater size, air conditioning, and a great deal of other facts. The listing service also allows for 20-30 pictures of your home. Once your real estate agent loads your information and sales price in the system, you can expect to start getting calls immediately.

If you use your local listing service understand that it might be required for you to pay a commission of 2%-3% to the buyer agent. Even if it is not required to pay a buyer commission, you should still offer a commission of at least 2% in order to make your listing attractive for real estate agents to show your home. I offered 3% commission on the sale of my home, and my strategy was that if the buyer was represented by a buyer agent, then I was not going to negotiate as much as I would with a buyer who did not have an agent.

Zillow:

In my experience I obtained roughly 15% of my leads from Zillow. It is a great tool to use for advertising your home for sale. Zillow enables you to create a whole profile of your home on their website for free. The Zillow profile is very similar to information that your real estate agent would enter into the listing service. The difference is that you as the homeowner have complete control over your home's profile and you don't need to involve a real estate agent.

The great thing about Zillow is that people are becoming increasingly aware of the website for obtaining the value of their home and are listing their home there for sale. Not only that, but a great many people are using Zillow as a first resource when they are in the market for a new home.

Zillow allows a person to zero in on an area of a city and view homes that sold, homes for sale, and homes not yet on the market. Zillow lists the Zestimate price for each home for each of its categories. It's a very useful tool for a buyer to use to determine where they want to live and compare homes that they are potentially interested in buying. I highly recommend using Zillow if you are a do-it-yourself home seller.

Facebook:

In my experience I obtained roughly 10% of my leads from Facebook. It is a great resource that every person selling their home the FSBO should use to maximize their advertising efforts. Facebook is becoming increasingly popular as a way to advertise a variety of interests, including selling your home.

The way that you advertise your home for sale on Facebook is to first join the group pages in the area. First look for your city and then join a real estate for sale group and possibly other groups that advertise things for sale. Then create a post in that group forum with the description of your home and its pictures.

As there is no form or structured way to advertise your home for sale, you will have to use your creativity to create this post and write the common things you think people are interested in knowing. You want to ensure that you list the number of bedrooms, bathrooms, living rooms, dining rooms, kitchens, and the home square footage. Next list your home's unique features and finer touches. List your address, school district, and the area of the city your home is in. Finally, you should list your home's selling price and your contact information.

Craigslist:

In my experience I obtained roughly 5% of my leads from Craigslist. I have to admit that I was a little disappointed with our results from Craigslist. I had the impression that Craigslist would have produced better results. Rather what I found is that most people didn't use Craigslist for home searching as much as I anticipated.

As it turns out Craigslist is more used for classified ads that are of simpler value. However, Craigslist produces some results that should not be ignored. Use Craigslist, but don't count on it alone to sell your home.

One caution that I should mention is that you will likely experience prank callers with Craigslist, and that you may get phone calls from unruly people. My wife and I experienced a rude caller who misrepresented herself in an untasteful way, which we easily calculated as a prank call. The bottom line is that if you post with Craigslist, ensure that you take caution with the callers. Have a predetermined script to weed out otherwise unscrupulous callers.

Open House:

In my experience we obtained roughly 10% of our leads from having an open house. We held an open house every weekend until we sold our home. It was an exciting experience to meet people who were interested in our home. It was also a great resource to gauge people's interest in the home considering the price we were asking.

Keep in mind that a successful house showing may only produce a single looker per day of open house. I would only recommend that you do an open house on Saturday and Sunday. I would not ordinarily expect that you would be able to show your home on other week days. There is a long held tradition that if there is an open house, it is normally on a Sunday. This is what the market is accustomed to, and you will likely have unfavorable results if you try to have an open house every day of the week. Instead, save your energy to have a perfectly performed open house on Saturday and Sunday when it is ordinarily expected.

Make sure that the house is clean, that the house smells good, and that the house is properly staged. Holding your open house on a Saturday or Sunday or both will lead to some prospective buyers. Have an open mind about hosting an open house: it could generate a lot of interest, or it may not be as much as you hoped for, but consider an open house successful if at least one person came to see your home.

As mentioned above, hosting your own open house lets you engage with potential buyers and gain an understanding of what may be holding back other buyers from making an offer if you have had multiple lookers and no takers.

From the comments and interactions with people you might gain a perspective of something you overlooked that needs fixing. Some things you may be able to fix, and others you may not be able to fix. Most people however will only tell you what they liked and might not give you the constructive feedback that you are looking for.

If you have an open house, make it as professional as possible. Have everything in place, picture perfect and be patient. Have your sign-in roster ready. Hope for a busy day of showing, but count it a success if at least one or two people show up for the open house.

It's useful to have a sign-in roster for multiple reasons. First, if you decide to lower the price of your home you might want to contact people on that list that might change their mind about buying your home. Second, if there is someone interested in buying your home, and they make an offer less than your asking price, you might want to contact previous lookers to let them know that you have just received an offer and were curious if they might be interested in making an offer as well. If you get more than one person bidding on your home, the result will be in your favor for landing a higher selling price.

Signage:

Signage is important for selling your home, but it very much varies on where you home is located. If your home is on a busy street, then be assured that a sign will make all the difference in the world. If your home is on a silent street or a cul-de-sac, then it might not be much of a big deal. In my case, I had a home in a cul-de-sac and did not put up a sign and was under contract to sell our home within 30 days.

I am certain that if you live on a busy street a sign will do you very good. At least people who are looking at other places in your neighborhood would likely see your home for sale and be interested in seeing your home.

Newspaper:

I feel that your local newspaper may still be a resource for gaining additional leads. However, I am not convinced that it is necessary. I feel that it is necessary that you list in the other methods listed above. However, there are still people who check the classifieds in the newspaper, and might find your home based on the paper. The number of people who check the paper as a resource these days is declining but not yet depreciated.

I did not use the paper as a resource for selling my home in 30 days, so I cannot comment on its effectiveness. I would imagine that it will produce leads, but am uncertain about how many. It might produce as much as another 5% to 10% more leads, so you will have to decide if that is worth your time, effort, and money.

Use the companion website at http://www.realestate-forsalebyowner.com to find additional resources about advertising your home.

Step Seven: Show

Time Involved: (1 week–3 months)

If by now you are ready to show your home, then you might have questions about what happens next. This chapter is designed to guide your through the process of showing your home. In the next chapters I will walk you through the offer and acceptance and contract on your home and through the closing on your home.

This stage of selling my home was one of the most frightening experiences that I had in the course of selling my home. I wasn't experienced and wasn't sure what I was doing or getting myself into. I was concerned about leaving my house, and letting strangers come and visit without me there. I was concerned about how to interact with real estate agents and what I should say. I ended up diving into the process without knowing, without guidance, and with great uncertainty. I learned some things along the way that I share with you below. I hope that this takes some of the edge off any uncertainty, if there is any uneasiness.

Lock Box:

A lock box or keypad entry system is absolutely necessary, and it is the first thing you must purchase before you begin to show your home. It is important because your potential buyers want anonymity when they come to see your home. They want to view your home without having to meet and greet with you person to person. This makes the buyers uncomfortable in thoroughly inspecting the home. They want to open the closets, the kitchen cabinets, pantry, and all your closed doors. With anonymity they feel free to do these things. If they meet you, then it's more personal and they may feel like they are intruding on your space. Worse off, if you insist on being present during the showing, then they will feel that they are being watched and hovered over.

The lock box or keypad entry system allows you to show your home without your presence. The lock box allows you to put a house key in a box that hangs on the outside of your door. You set the code for the box, and you give that code to the real estate agents that are showing your home.

A keypad entry system is a nice upgrade to your home if you decide to purchase one. The keypad entry system is built into the door deadbolt, and can be opened with a pin. This is a nice way to improve the appeal of your home, and is the first thing people will notice when they come to view your home.

Sign-in Sheets:

It is a good practice to ask everyone who views your home to sign in when viewing your home. Place the sign-in sheet close to the entry of the home if possible or in the kitchen on the table or counter. It's a good tool that you can use for multiple purposes. First, you can easily tally up if you are hitting your numbers for showing your place. Recall that if you are showing your home three to five times a week, then you are priced about right. Second, it shows others how many people have viewed your place. This could create the feeling of competition in your potential buyers. Third, if you are not making your numbers and are possibly considering lowering your price, then you can call the potential buyers and see if they would be interested in your home at a lower price. Fourth, after a showing, you can call the real estate agent of the buyer and ask them for their opinion about your home, and if there was something that should be improved.

A sign-in sheet should be printed and professional looking. It should include the date, time, the buyer agent's name, phone number, and email, and the buyer's name, phone number, and email. You can request more information if you would like, but it's best to keep this as short as possible as many people won't want to spend a lot of time filling in too many details.

Home Fact Sheet:

A home fact sheet is a flyer that you give to potential buyers. Leave these in a noticeable spot in the same location as the sign-in sheets. This flyer should be in color and have about three of the best pictures of your home on it. Include the address, school district, and subdivision for describing the location. Include a sales pitch about the home that describes the home's finer features and amenities. Keep the flyer to one page only. Someone should be able to read it rapidly, and understand what is unique about the home.

A flyer is a great way to keep your home at the top of someone's mind. The potential buyer takes this with them and has something with them to remind them about viewing your home when comparing to other homes. Potential buyers might look at ten to twenty homes before making a decision to buy your home, and when looking at this many homes, it becomes difficult to remember your home's finer features. The flyer helps remind people what it was about your home that they liked.

Business Cards:

If your home is being showed by a real estate agent then I would recommend that you request that the agent also leave behind a business card. This is useful for a number of reasons. If the real estate agent does not sign in on your sign-in sheet, then they might be more inclined to leave their card. If they leave their card, then make a follow up call with them and ask how the showing went. As stated before, ask them if something should be improved upon. Ask if the house was staged well and felt clean. Ask if there is anything holding the buyers back from purchasing your property.

Armed with the answers to your questions, ask yourself if there is something that you could improve. If the agent says that that bathroom seemed dirty, can you spruce it up and freshen it somehow? If the agent says that the buyer wanted a bigger kitchen, just take it with a grain of salt and understand that it is something that you can't change. Be positive and keep the belief that someone will find your kitchen is perfect for them. Everyone has different tastes and different needs. Your home is perfect for someone. The feedback you are looking for is what did not show well that you can fix, such as cleaning or re-organizing.

Checking on Real Estate Agent Credentials:

Here is a trick that most For-Sale-by-Owners don't know about. You can check on the real estate agents credentials using the internet. You can use your favorite search engine to find free resources for checking credentials. All you have to do is enter in basic information about the agent to search the database to make sure that someone that calls you is indeed a licensed real estate agent. When I learned this, it gave me a huge peace of mind knowing that if an agent is shows my house that I had a way to check that they were in fact a licensed real estate agent. Another thing that I learned is that there are laws and statutes that govern a real estate agent's behavior, and that they have a fiduciary responsibility when showing your home. The real estate agent is responsible for their buyer's actions. For instance if the buyer causes some damage to your home as a result of the real estate agent's showing your home then the agent and buyer can be held responsible for making the necessary repairs.

It's worth your time to check the credentials of every real estate agent who shows your home and keep a record of the real estate agent's ID. Write the information down and keep it in your records. Check the information to ensure that they are not misrepresenting themselves.

There are two types of showings that you need to be concerned about. First, there is the showing that is chaperoned by a real estate agent. The second is the showing of a buyer without a real estate agent. Since you are selling your home in a non-traditional fashion, either strictly on your own or with the help of a flat-fee real estate agent, in either case you will need to schedule your own showings. This is not very difficult, but a little more work is involved when you are not using a conventional real estate agent. Each type of showing deserves a discussion and I will address each below.

When a real estate agent is involved, make sure that you answer the phone in a professional manner. When you answer the phone from an unrecognized number, answer the phone with, "Hello this is (your name). How may I help you?," rather than just saying hello! Be polite and courteous to every caller, and anticipate that it is a real estate agent calling to schedule the showing of your home. When the call is from a real estate agent, get the date and time they want to show your home and make every opportunity to allow them to show your home at the time they request. If the requested time is dinner time for you and your family, then possibly take the family out for the night. Personally I allowed every showing to happen at the buyer's requested time.

If you run into the case where multiple real estate agents want to show your home at the same time, let them know that you have another real estate agent scheduled for the same time and they are welcome to show at that time if their client does not mind that another buyer may be looking at the same time. This can work out advantageously for you if the buyers sense competition in buying your home.

If the potential buyer does not have a real estate agent, then you have a sweet advantage when it comes to the sale of your property. This means that potentially you won't be paying a buyer commission, and on top of that, not paying a seller commission either, ka-ching! However, there is more risk involved in allowing someone to view your home without a buyer real estate agent. The buyer has little responsibility for you and you will have less recourse in the case of losses or damages. The next paragraph will give you some ideas on how you might mitigate the risks involved.

Once you have learned that the buyer does not have a real estate agent, ask them if they would be interested in coming to your open house. Let them know that you don't have a real estate selling agent to show them your home and that your are selling the home yourself. If your next open house does not work for them, then you have one other option, which is to show your home yourself.

When you show your own home, I recommend taking a few precautions before the showing. Remove any items from your home that are valuable and easily concealable. Either put these things in the car or store them in an area of the house that can be locked separately. At the time of showing, make sure you welcome your guests with a friendly smile and tell them to feel free to look at your home. Take a moment to upsell some of the features of the home, and give a sales pitch. Keep the pitch short, ask them to sign in, then I would recommend letting them go inside while you wait outside. Resist the urge to follow them throughout the house. Let them feel comfortable and unwatched. If you stay inside during the showing then make sure you stay in an area where the guests will feel unwatched. The buyers want to look over the home and see all the spaces and storage. If you are there watching them, they won't feel comfortable opening closets, cabinets, and closed doors. It's important to people to see that your home will have plenty of storage for their needs.

Use the companion website at http://www.realestate-forsalebyowner.com to find additional resources about showing your home.

Step Eight: Offer and Acceptance and Contract

Time Involved: (1 month or less)

Showing your home successfully and following the steps in this book will inevitably lead to the sale of your home. This is an exciting time for you, and you are about to breathe a sigh of relief: you are one step closer to selling your home. This chapter will walk you through the steps from the offer up to closing day.

This is the stage of selling your home at which a flat-fee real estate professional can be really helpful in navigating through all the documents required to move toward closing. Real estate agents can't and won't practice law so you may want to engage your own attorney at this point to protect your specific personal interests as to the documents or the transaction, but forms and documents available through real estate agents are a good starting point. Often the flat-fee real estate professional's services are or can be included in the price you paid to have them list you on real estate directories. In my experience, my flat-fee real estate professional was very helpful at this stage of the process. He thoroughly explained everything that was about to happen and could articulate whether the offer conformed to normal conventions. When I decided to counter-offer the buyer's initial offer my real estate agent gave me constructive advice on how I might structure the counter. The creative solution he gave me was to accept their selling price, but take my appliances that were originally listed as part of the sale. This in effect met the buyer's offer halfway. This resulted in the buyer happily accepting my counter.

If you haven't already purchased services from a flat-fee real estate professional then I strongly urge you to obtain the services they provide, or engage with a real estate attorney as I mentioned above, who can advise you on how your legal rights are affected by the contractual documents and procedures. The companion website at (website) can connect you with a flat-fee real estate agent and attorney that provides these services at reasonable prices.

Offer and Counter-offer:

When you get an offer on your home, it's a moment filled with anticipation and excitement. As you begin to read the offer the first thing you will want to do is jump to how much the offer is for. Based on the offer, a range of other emotions may settle in. This is completely natural; keep a calm and cool head as you review the initial offer, whether it is favorable or not. Remember that it is an offer, it's not a contract until you and the buyer agree to all the terms and you sign your acceptance which then creates a contract.

The initial offer will have a number of items in it, most of the items are fairly standard. Of course there is the actual price, which most people are most concerned about. Then there are a number of deadline dates for the steps that bring you to closing. For instance there are normally deadlines set for title work, homeowners association, property disclosure, loan application, appraisal, survey, inspection, and closing objections. These are all timelines that you and the buyer are agreeing to in the transaction. Any of these items could end up with an objection by the buyer or seller.

The offer may be countered by the seller if the seller feels that some of the terms of the contract need adjusting. For instance, the seller might counter on price if the offered price was too low. The seller might also counter on dates if the dates don't conform or cannot be supported by the seller for some reason.

It's important to know that during this period of offer and counter-offer that contract laws on offer and acceptance apply and a lawyer should be consulted for a specific discussion of legal rights where either party might object to what was offered or counter-offered or want to withdraw or cancel the proceedings.

Contract:

You have a contract when both you the seller and the buyer agree to the terms of the sale as mentioned above. You both agree to the price, other terms, and the deadlines of the transaction. Often times listing services will report your property as being under contract. However, the contract includes terms about the steps to be taken toward closing, many of which have requirements and contingencies that could cause or allow the contract to be canceled along the way. The contract terms can be looked as providing a "to do" list or road map to closing. Signing the contract does not mean that things are finalized.

After signing the contract, understand that all of the deadline items may result in further negotiation before closing. One such example is that it is common for the buyer to object to some or all items in the inspection report and may request certain items in the report to be corrected by the seller. A seller might object to the request and counter the objection with their own offer, which is basically another round of negotiation with provisions in the contract for what happens if the parties don't reach an agreement. Another example that occurs less often is that the buyer could also object to the price of the home if the home is not appraised to be of the amount offered in the contract. Finally, keep in mind that the buyer could cancel the contract based on not getting favorable loan conditions.

You should know that there are many items that could be objected to within the timelines agreed. If the objections are made within the timelines then these objections might spark further negotiation and amendments to the contract. Parties may also request an amendment to the contract to agree to modifications in an agreed-to deadline, but "time is of the essence" in real estate contracts, so both parties need to be diligent on dates and deadlines and no request for an amendment is guaranteed.

Addendums and Disclosures:

There are a number of items that may also be required by your state to include as addendums or disclosures. Some of these may include an estimate of expenses at closing, closing instructions, property condition disclosure, radon/microbials and other environmental pollutants, criminal offenders registry, square footage disclosure, lead-based paint disclosure, and a variety of others. State requirements will vary, so you need to check to see what state requirements may exist in your state. The following paragraphs explain some of the more common ones I have mentioned.

The closing instructions is normally a part of the contract or an addendum to the contract that spells out how the closing will proceed. This is usually a straightforward process, as once you as a seller choose a title company the title company will provide the instructions for closing. As the seller, you are normally the one who chooses the title company as the title company fees are paid by you the seller. Another similar addendum may include estimates of expenses at closing for both the seller and buyer.

The property disclosure is a key document often in the form of a checklist with blanks for explanation that is required for the seller to complete and submit to the buyer either before the offer or just after the offer. This could be included at showing and made available to prospective buyers or will take place just after the offer depending on your state requirements, and gives the seller a chance to explain a discrepancy of the home that the seller may be aware of that they are disclosing to the buyer. This is a very important disclosure with the seller disclosing and explaining details of the property and its condition. Generally a disclosure form will ask the seller to disclose any known defects in the home that they are aware of. It will ask of any warranties that may be transferrable with the home. Finally, it will ask about utilities and existing homeowners associations and other matters about the residence and property. It is most important that the seller be truthful with all answers in this document in all matters. If you don't know something, don't just say yes or not, write in "don't know". Be thorough.

The square footage disclosure is a document that asks you to certify to the best of you knowledge the square footage of the home. Normally it is a document that does not guarantee the square footage but exercise care to minimize any discrepancy in what the actual square footage is. Sometimes the square footage is reported on the county appraiser's website. The property inspector, insurance company, and the bank appraiser should check these numbers by measuring the dimensions themselves.

If you own an older home built before 1978 it is required that you provide a warning statement in your contract about lead-based paint. Plus you need to provide a lead hazard information pamphlet; disclose the presence of any known lead-based paint or hazards and copies of inspections or assessments; and permit the buyer a 10 day period to inspect. You should have the buyer sign a statement that the buyer received the warning pamphlet. This is an important but simple form explaining what you know and providing copies or stating that you have no knowledge or reports. The Environmental Protection Agency (EPA) pamphlet "Protect Your Family from Lead in Your Home" can be downloaded at: http://www.hud.gov/offices/lead/library/enforcement/pyf_eng.pdf

Some states may require you to disclose whether the home has ever been used as a methamphetamine lab. The chemicals used to create methamphetamines are toxic to human health and there could be a requirement by your state to disclose any knowledge you may have about whether the home has ever been used as a methamphetamine lab.

Some states are requiring a disclosure about offender registries maintained by the state.

Keep copies with the signature of the buyer showing that the buyer has received these addendums and disclosures. Each state will have its own requirements so you will have to do your own checking on this or consult with a lawyer on this.

Pre-approved Finance Letter:

The buyer's pre-approved finance letter is a helpful document in the process of selling your home. The finance letter is an assurance that the buyer has reviewed finances with their lender and is expected to have the necessary finances and credit to purchase a property. The letter most likely has a variety of reservations and contingencies by the lender, so you should read the letter and include appropriate wording in your contract to make sure that the lender's requirements are met.

Home Inspection:

After the contract is completed and signed, the first step in working toward closing is most often the home inspection. Home inspections are a very common aspect of selling your home, and you should not worry much about the inspection. Home inspectors will inspect the home to report back to the buyer about the details of the condition of the home. They typically report about plumbing and whether they visibly saw any leaks under the sinks in the kitchen and bathrooms. They typically check all the outlets to ensure that they are wired correctly. They will check to see if the doors and windows operate properly. They check the condition of the roof, exterior of the home, and foundation. They will inspect the water heater, furnace, and central air of the home. Typically, inspectors are looking at the major systems of the home and aren't typically nit-noid about every little detail, scratch, or nail hole. It varies greatly from inspector to inspector on what they report on. The basic general rule in purchasing real estate is "buyer beware," so buyers do want their inspectors to be thorough. Contracts then usually provide for negotiation on what to do with exceptions reported by the inspector, with various terms on responding with negotiation, reduction in price, take "as is" or rights to terminate in either party.

Radon Test:

Radon tests are becoming more and more common to be included in the home inspection. A radon test measures the amount of radon gas present in your home to determine if the level is safe for living. Radon is a gas that is present naturally and seeps into the home from the soil. If your home has radon above the prescribed threshold, then normally the buyer will insist on radon mitigation. This could involve installing a ventilation system in the flooring of your home to expel the gas. Typically ventilation systems can cost somewhere between $500 and $3000.

Foundation Inspection:

If the home inspection raises concerns about the foundation, the buyer may further do a foundation inspection. The buyer's foundation inspector will inspect the foundation and determine if there is concern about the foundation. If the concerns are minor, then the inspector will likely recommend that nothing be done. If the concerns are more serious in nature then they might recommend that the foundation be fixed. No one wants to hear that there is a foundation issue with the sale of their home, and it may cause excessive worry. If it is determined that there is a foundation issue, don't fret overly about it. Most foundation issues can be corrected for less than $5000. If you feel the price of the foundation repair is excessive, remember that you can negotiate with the buyer. You might offer to pay half of the cost rather than footing the entire bill.

Bank Appraisal:

The bank appraisal is normally the last step involved before the closing of the home. Nearly all banks will require an appraisal of your home as a condition of providing a loan to the buyers. The appraisal is charged to the buyer and an appraisal will be required regardless of whether you have already hired your own appraiser and have the appraisal report in hand.

Again, this is not something to worry about. the appraiser is there to make a report and express the appraiser's opinion on the fair market value of the property. Generally, the fair market value of a home is what a reasonable buyer and seller are willing to negotiate in the terms of a transaction. The fact that you are a reasonable seller, and assuming the buyer is a reasonable buyer, then the price that the two of you negotiated should be expected to be at or close to what an appraiser's report would independently conclude as the fair market value of your home. The appraiser will consider various factors and study nearby comparable sales in coming up with the opinion of fair market value.

Step Nine: Title and Closing

Time Involved: (1 week)

Title Company:

As the seller you typically will make arrangements with a title company to handle a title commitment, closing, and title policy for the property. The title company can't practice law so they won't prepare legal documents. Their title commitment will outline the encumbrances on the property and also steps to be taken to close so that they are in a position to provide their title insurance policy to the buyer. They may be helpful in referring you to an attorney or sometimes a title company will has a package of common forms or statutory forms that can be used. The title company can also handle closing. In doing so, the title company will do such things as obtain the payoff information from your mortgage company; calculate any real estate sales commissions; calculate any taxes that are involved with the sale of your home; and calculate any other charges that may be involved, such as a homeowner warranty or other charges to the seller or buyer. There is a title company closing fee that is generally split between the seller and the buyer.

The title company generally serves as an escrow for deposits and payments made under the contract. For closing, the title company makes sure that the releases have been filed for any liens being cleared by the seller so that insurance can be issued. The title company also calculates the property tax that is owed by the seller, if any. If a Homeowner's Association (HOA) is involved then they make sure that the seller has obtained a letter or other proof dues are up to date. To summarize, at closing the title company calculates all the matters from the contract involved with the sale of your home and ensures that, upon transfer of the home from the seller to the buyer, the deed is subject only to the exceptions listed in the title commitment. The title company insures based on the filed record. There may be unknown liens or debts owed against the property but any claim by the buyer on those will have to be made back against the seller.

The title transfer fees are normally paid for by the seller, and as such normally the seller chooses which title company is used to process the transfer. There is normally more than one title company in a given city; however, some smaller townships may only have one or none at all, and you may have to reach out to a city nearby to close on the sale of your home.

If the buyer has a lender, the lender will close its own loan and provide funds and paperwork to the title company to record.

You can help your title company if you are able to provide the title company a copy of your old title insurance policy. Ask if the existing policy might qualify you for a discount on the new policy.

Loan Payoff:

This is an important topic to write about and warrants its own section, because the title company must have the loan payoff information in order to close on your home. The title company normally obtains this information directly from your mortgage company. However, the buck really stops at you to be involved with this process. Sometimes mortgage companies don't play nice and it may be difficult for your title company to obtain the payoff information. Have the expectation that you might have to become personally involved. You might have to call the mortgage company yourself to get the payoff information for your title company. I would suggest that the title company orders the payoff information no less than two weeks prior to closing, and that you personally check that the title company has the payoff information no less than five days prior to closing. Some banks will insist on having three days to process the payoff request and that the day of the request does not count. So if you are to close on time then you want to make sure that the title company has the payoff information the day prior to closing, which means that you should check with the title company no less than five days prior to closing.

Buyer's Closing Costs:

The major buyer closing expenses and costs normally are associated with obtaining a loan. These expenses and costs normally include application fees, appraisal fees, prepayment of taxes and insurance into a lender escrow, and other filing fees and settlement charges.

Seller's Closing Costs:

The seller also has closing expenses and costs. First there is the buying real estate agent's commission, if you offered one. It's recommended at the time of writing this book that you offer a buyer real estate agent commission and list your home on a real estate listing service in your state. However, this will come at the cost of two or three percent of the sale of your home, depending on the commission you set. This commission will be paid at closing.

Second, there is a fee for the owner's title policy (buyer pays its own mortgagee's title policy to insure a lender); generally ½ of the title company's closing fee. There may be other charges such as a wire fee for money transfers or other miscellaneous items.

Finally, there may be fees associated with your own mortgage company pay off. Further, you need to advance pay the buyer for your share of the current year's property taxes, which the buyer will have to pay in full at the end of the year or tax period. There could also be other fees depending on your state.

Final Walk-thru Inspection:

It is customary for the buyer to walk through the house the day prior to closing. This is to allow the buyer to re-inspect to see that there were no damages caused by the seller in the move out process. This is not typically a thorough process like the home inspection. This is simply the buyer checking that any agreements in the contract for repairs were met, and that the home is delivered as expected.

I would recommend that not only the place be repaired according to the agreement, but also that an appropriate amount of time be spent cleaning the home. You would not want to surprise the new owner with a ton of cleaning that is required for them to move into their new home. Although it may not be mentioned in the contract, it's a courtesy that I think everyone should pass on to a buyer who in good faith bought your home.

Receipts:

Ensure that you bring with you to closing all of the receipts for fees you paid in the course of making repairs or other mitigations that were agreed to in the contract and paid. Otherwise, failure to show proof that you have met the contractual agreements could delay your closing. For this reason I recommend bringing these to the title company on the day of closing.

By bringing the paid receipts to closing, the receipts can be included in the title company's closing file when closing on the home.

Day of Closing:

On the day of closing make sure that you dress appropriately for the occasion. Formal attire is not required, or expected, but you should dress in business casual, or in respectable attire. You can wear jeans and a polo shirt or button up shirt. The clothes should be neat, clean, and free of stains or holes.

Depending on the state you live in, the closing process could vary widely. In some states the buyer and seller meet face to face during the transfer of the home, while in other states the buyer and seller meet privately with only the title company on separate occasions. Oftentimes the seller will meet the day before or even handle it by mail.

Expect to sign and initial plenty of documents. The process should take about an hour, most of which is the buyer signing loan documents. At the end of the process, the recording of the deed, buyer's mortgage, and update of the title commitment for the title company to issue its title policy, title company will wire funds or write you a check for any proceeds owed to you, depending on your state. Possibly the opposite may be true: you may have to write a check for the amount that you owe in the transaction if you sold your home short of the amount owed or short of your closing fees.

During the time of closing, you will provide the new owner the keys to the home, and garage door openers if applicable. Also, this is a time to supplement any other considerations about the home such as how to care for certain things. You might discuss when garbage day is, and the unique rules about recycling. You might also share with the new owner tricks you learned for how to care for the grass, plants, trees or shrubs.

At the end of the closing, after signing all the documents and closing statements, the title company will make copies of everything you signed. After filings are made and the title commitment updated so that the policy is ready to issue, the title company will wire or mail you a check for any balance owed to you. Depending on the state, the title company might have a waiting period or might mail you the proceeds. That's it, closing is a fairly simple and straightforward process.

After the closing there are a few things left for you to ensure are taken care of. First, make sure that you forward your US mail to a new address, so that your mail is handled properly. Second, there will normally be some refunds due back to you from your mortgage company. Your mortgage company will be refunding you your escrow account if you have one. Also, if your insurance is not included in your loan escrow account, notify your insurance company to advise them of the transfer and request a refund of any unused portion of your insurance policy premium. You should take time to call these companies first to update them with a new address to send you these checks.

Concluding Thoughts

Using the FSBO method of selling your home is not as complicated as you may have believed it was before reading this book. The process is fairly simple if you know how to navigate through it. Using the FSBO methods described in the chapters of this book will lead you to save potentially thousands of dollars. Ensure that you use my companion website at http://www.realestat-forsalebyowner.com for additional resources that were not mentioned in this book. I have compiled a check list and other articles and documents that you can consider using in the course of selling your home.

My goal with this book was to help others who want to use the FSBO method of selling their home, but may have been unsure where to start. Further, I hope that reading this book was a great start for putting you on your path to selling your home yourself. I hope that I have demystified some of the questions you may have had, and that if there was something holding your back, you are abundantly more confident that you can do it!

First Edition 2014

www.ingramcontent.com/pod-product-compliance
Lightning Source LLC
Chambersburg PA
CBHW051734170526
45167CB00002B/933